Record Keeping Made Easy

7 Steps To Getting More Done With Less Stress
For Probation Practitioners

Sonia Harris

First published in the UK 2016 by Sonia Harris

Copyright © Sonia Harris 2016

ISBN-13: 978-1539774495

Contents

Acknowledgements   vii

Foreword   ix

Introduction   xiii

Chapter 1: So Why Record?   1

Chapter 2: Write It Now and Save Time Later   11

Chapter 3: What to Put In and What to Leave Out   23

Chapter 4: Sonia's PAP™Record-Keeping System   39

Chapter 5: Get More Done at Work and

        Enjoy Your Life at Home   47

Chapter 6: How to Be Tech Savvy   57

Chapter 7: How to Tame Your Email Inbox   67

Conclusion   83

References   85

Dedicated to my mum, Joyce Harris, who was my number one supporter and sadly died before this book was published.

Acknowledgements

I would like to thank Raymond Aaron and his team for planting the seed that set me on the journey to write this book.

I would like to thank Judy Cullins for guidance in helping me to identify the core purpose of this book.

I am grateful to family, friends and colleagues who have provided feedback and encouragement.

Foreword

You may have picked up this book out of curiosity because you work directly with service users, or supervise staff that do. You may be very experienced and feel that you are very skilled at case recording, and you may be right. Or you may be very new in your organisation and not feel very confident about a number of tasks, case recording just being one of them. Whatever your reasons for picking up this book, I urge you not to put it down until you have answered these four questions:

1. Have you received any training on case recording? That is, have you been taught about what you should record and what you shouldn't?
2. Do you consistently follow a clear structure when you record so that colleagues fully understand what is going on in your case?
3. Do you know whether or not your recording practice is within the law?
4. Are your case records always clear, accurate and up to date?

If your answer is no to any of the above three questions, *Record Keeping Made Easy: 7 Steps To Get More Done With Less Stress* by Sonia Harris is intended to provide you with the key principles in effective case recording. The book will help you to evaluate your current practice. You will learn strategies to improve and simplify your record keeping so that it is more accurate, simple to read and concise. Now that service users have access to their records, it is important that your records are fit for purpose and stay within legislative requirements.

In your kind of work, you know the importance of good communication, both oral and written, and that this is constantly under scrutiny. There is an increasing demand to provide written evidence of what you do, and a requirement to data input for monitoring purposes. It is not surprising that you feel that face-to-face time with service users is being squeezed, and you no doubt find yourself saying, "This isn't what I signed up for."

This is a plain-speaking book that will offer you some immediate insights, and will immediately have an impact on your record keeping practice. Once read, you will want to keep it handy because it will act as a constant guide. I will also say that, once you are familiar with the principles of effective case recording, you will want to share them with your colleagues.

Sonia Harris is passionate about helping you to be the best that you can be. When she learns something new, she has an overwhelming desire to share the information if she feels it would be of benefit to you.

Raymond Aaron
New York Times Best-selling author of Chicken Soup for the Parent's Soul

Introduction

Do you fall behind with your record keeping and spend hours trying to catch up?

Do you start work early and stay late just so that you can stay on top of your work?

Do you postpone taking your annual leave because you are not up-to-date with your case records?

Are you so overwhelmed at work that when you are at home you worry about what you have not done?

Do you wake up suddenly at night because you forgot to record vital information in a case record?

If this sounds like you, you will discover how the simple strategies in this book will immediately improve the quality of your record keeping. This book is also for support staff and administrators who will feel more confident about how and what they should write in a case record. Managers can also use this book to help staff who struggle with keeping their case records up-to-date.

Record Keeping Made Easy: 7 Steps To Get More Done With Less Stress For Probation Practitioners will help you elevate your record keeping from a laborious administrative task to a positive and fulfilling professional tool. Inside this book you will find:

- 3 Tips to help you to prioritise your case recording.

- 10 Steps To Faster, Easy To Write Record Keeping.

- 9 Simple actions you can take to make your case records easy to understand.

- What layout you can use to make your case records easier to read.

- 7 time stealers and how you can avoid them.

- 5 Work-life balance mistakes and what you can do about them so you feel happier and less distracted.

- How you can reduce your stress and increase your resilience.

- Some tech savvy tips to reduce computer stress

- 5 Easy steps to getting control over your email inbox.

I wrote this book to give back some control to those Practitioners who have too much work and too little time. They are forced to prioritise other tasks over record keeping because they are too busy fire fighting. By the time they get around to writing up their case records, they are often drained and stressed out. They begin to see case recording as a time-consuming administrative task instead of an integral part of their professional work.

At the age of 15 I told the careers adviser that I wanted to be a probation officer or teacher. He told me that I would not suit either profession. As a probation officer I would have to be able to stand up in court and speak before a judge. As a teacher I would have to stand in front of a class of children and teach. He told me that he thought I was too shy and I believed him. As I had an interest in needlework he suggested I consider textile and design.

So at 18 I went off to Huddersfield to do a BSc in Textile Design with a new dream of becoming a designer. I lasted less than six months. Despite being a single mother I started a BEd degree the following year and qualified as a teacher at the age of 23. My dream of becoming a teacher had been realised. I do remember having to keep records on my children and providing end of year reports.

When my daughter was about to start school I made the decision to move to part-time work so that I could be around more for her at the start and finish of school. I would probably have carried on teaching if I had been able to find a part-time position, but I found myself applying and accepting a crèche worker job just because I needed a job and that was available at the time.

That started my journey within the voluntary sector. I progressed from that job to working as a child care worker in a women's refuge. I still had a desire to work with children and had decided I preferred the more informal working environment of the voluntary sector, rather than the formal setting of a school.

It wasn't until I moved on to take up a position as a senior youth worker in a youth centre that I was required to keep records and provide monthly reports to a management committee. I also learnt how to prepare funding proposals and provide reports to the local council, demonstrating that the money we'd been given had been spent wisely.

Threatened with redundancy I had to think about what I wanted to do next. I remembered that I'd once thought about being a probation officer. At that time my best friend was working as a probation officer and so I decided to apply to pursue a diploma in social work, which was the requirement at that time.

I was successful in securing a place but not for the probation pathway. I decided to take a job working in a probation hostel and re-apply the following year. It was whilst working as a hostel worker that I understood the importance of good quality record keeping. At the start of my shift I would read the "Day book" to update myself on what had happened since I was last there. Sometimes this was easy to do but at other times it was a struggle to comprehend what had been written.

When I re-applied the following year I was successful in getting a place on the probation pathway of the Diploma in Social Work programme. During my training I worked in a social work department and that was first experience of case work within a statutory care department. I found out how challenging it could be balancing the time needed to work directly with service users and then providing a written account of those contacts for the organisation's records.

In 1996 I got a job as a qualified probation officer and worked in a generic team for 5 years. I remember times feeling relieved when a service user failed to keep an appointment because it gave me time to catch up on my case records.

I then worked as a practice development assessor for 7 years. I enjoyed training and supporting trainee probation officers through their National Vocational Qualification. Now I was in the position of reviewing and assessing the work of trainees. It was during this period that I really noticed the inconsistency in the quality of case records.

During this time I was successful in becoming a foster carer and over a 4 year period my family was responsible for giving a home to a total of 7 children. Although I was very aware of the importance of keeping good records it was the experience of being a foster carer that brought home how essential it is to keep contemporaneous notes.

I have spoken to family members in other professions, such as nursing, social care and housing, who describe very similar challenges when it comes to record keeping practices. Some people are very organised and always seem to be up to date with their record keeping. Others struggle with this task and so procrastinate, which only makes the situation worse.

I am somewhere in the middle. There are times when I am completely up to date with my records. During those times I feel of sense of lightness. I feel on top of everything. I feel I can deal with anything that is thrown at me. However, there have been times when I got totally overwhelmed with the amount of paperwork.

There was always a common issue. For some reason I had not kept up to date with my record keeping. As a foster carer it just meant putting off writing up the daily contacts, and then feeling totally overwhelmed. This would be aggravated if the child we were looking after was particularly challenging and left us exhausted. The last thing you want to do is sit down and write out a full account of what happened.

In my early years as a probation officer I struggled with keeping up to date with recording. That is when I invested in a book "Get Everything Done and Still Have Time to Play" by Mark Forster. I did not have access to that book during the writing of this because I'd lent it to one of my trainees years ago. However, just as I was coming to the end of this book the trainee, now a manager, returned the book to me.

I then read "The 7 Habits of Highly Effective People" by Stephen Covey. It was this book that changed my perspective and taught me new habits on how to manage me rather than my work.

More recently I've read "Getting Things Done: How To Achieve Stress-Free Productivity" by David Allen. You can see that I have an interest in productivity and stress management. So in this book I've brought the two together under the heading of record keeping.

Those of us who work in organisations where we support people with difficulties or who are ill are expected to demonstrate what we do and how we do it. Record keeping is the main way that this is done but unfortunately can often feel like a chore rather than a useful tool.

I wrote this book because I believe that record keeping is less stressful and time-consuming if you employ the right mindset and tools.

So are you ready to find out why it's important that you understand your responsibilities in keeping accurate and up-to-date records?

Chapter 1

So Why Record?

Do you worry about remembering all the information you receive on a case?

Do you have a way of evidencing the work you've done with service users?

In this chapter we look at why it is important that you understand your responsibilities when recording information about the service users you work with. It's been my experience that some practitioners do not fully appreciate this responsibility. They do not fully appreciate the adverse impact on themselves and the organisation if they fall foul of relevant legislation.

Is Good Record Keeping Really Necessary?

Statutory services are required to keep case records that are both accurate and up-to-date. A record should tell the reader what has been happening in a case: the what, why, when, who and how, including the decision-making process. The reader, of course, will be anyone in the organisation authorised to have access, as well as third party organisations and of course the service user.

Creating and maintaining case records is a crucial task and also takes up a lot of your time.

"When practitioners have written a communication and it has been considered by others or presented to decision-making fora, that document is then deemed to be a permanent record and cannot be changed. It will be filed in a case file and may be used as evidence in courts or tribunals." (Aberdeen City Council and Robert Gordon University, 2010)

What are the Benefits?

- Evidence of what you have done, how you have done it and when you did it
- You can see any gaps in contact
- Protects both you and the service user in the case of any legal or ethical proceedings
- Provides accountability to you and your organisation
- If questioned on any actions, you can refer to your records to show the rationale behind your decisions
- You stop using your mind for storage and avoid forgetting vital information

- Provides evidence of the organisation meeting any statutory requirements
- Can use records to monitor adherence to policies
- Offers accountability during audits

If you suddenly took ill and had to take time off work, would your colleagues be able to pick up one of your cases and know exactly what was happening with that case at that time?

The responsibility of writing records belongs to anyone who has information to give, or receives information relating to a case. This is from the receptionist who answers a telephone query to the director dealing with a service user complaint.

Service users have access to their records so it is important that whatever facts you record are accurate and clear. You may be confused about what information you can and cannot share. It is important that you understand the legislation associated with this area.

Both practitioners and service users can be confused when they find out that information, that they believed to be confidential, has been shared with a third party.

I remember when I worked in a bail and probation hostel in London I took a call from someone who wanted me to give them the personal telephone number of a colleague. This person insisted that they were a friend of my colleague and could not understand why I would not take her word for it. As far as I was concerned, all I had was a voice at the other end of the telephone. I had never spoken to this person before and for all I knew my colleague might not want this person to have their number for a range of reasons. I based my decision not to give out a personal number on the fact that I would not want one of my colleagues giving out my number to anyone without first having my permission.

Why You Can't Keep Secrets

When a service user discloses sensitive information - When you build rapport with a service user they can get comfortable and disclose more information with you than they intended. Once the information is out, it is out and cannot be taken back. If you do not clearly explain the meaning of confidentiality to service users, they can sometimes become angry and distressed if they later find out you shared that information with a third party. This is often in the case when child safeguarding issues are identified and you share information with social services or the police.

How to avoid (minimise) angry service users

- Inform service users at the very start how information about them is stored and what information will be shared with third parties
- Be very clear about what type of information that you have to share with third party agencies such as social services and police.

Sharing confidential information electronically or verbally

Information can be shared in many different formats. In addition to written correspondence and the telephone, information is now transmitted via email, texting, instant messaging and social media. Any information relating to the work you do with service users must never be shared via social media such as Facebook, Twitter, Instagram, Pinterest etc.

The main consideration is that, once you have passed information to someone else using any one of these media, you cannot be 100% sure the information has remained 100% confidential.

How to avoid accidently sharing confidential information to a third party when using the telephone

A simple telephone call can have numerous implications when it comes to confidentiality. When talking to someone on the telephone about a confidential matter, there are a number of issues you may need to consider.

Ask these questions when you are on the telephone

- Can anyone else outside that conversation hear what you are saying? Use a private room and close the door
- Is there a third party present with the person on the other end of the telephone that you don't know about? Confirm that the other person is on their own, is in a private room, and that the call is not on loud speaker.
- Is the call being recorded without your knowledge? If appropriate, clearly state that the conversation is confidential to the parties involved in the telephone call.
- Is the other person taking notes? Confirm that the notes will be stored privately and not shared with third parties who are not authorised to access the information.

Some people misunderstand the purpose of the Data Protection Act 1998 or confuse it with The Freedom of Information Act 1997.

The Data Protection Act is not about stopping you from sharing information. It is about ensuring that when you do share personal information, it is done appropriately. Individuals have the right to privacy; however, this has to be balanced against the benefits of sharing information, whether that is to safeguard children or vulnerable adults or to protect the public.

The Freedom of Information Act 1997 relates to the right of the public to access any recorded information held by public authorities.

The Seven Golden Rules For Information Sharing

1   The Data Protection Act is not meant to be a barrier to sharing information. However, it is important that any information that is shared about an individual is done so in an appropriate manner.

2   It is important to ensure openness and honesty with people so that they are very clear and understand what and how information about them will be shared. Where possible it is good practice to seek agreement but this may not be possible in some cases where the protection of the public or child safeguarding issues are apparent.

3   Whenever you have any doubts as to whether it is safe to share certain information it is always best to seek advice first if this is possible.

4   It is always a judgement call when deciding whether or not to share confidential information. This can be particularly complicated when an individual does not give consent to information about them being shared. However, their wishes may be overridden if in your judgement information needs to be shared in the public interest.

5   You may need to give careful consideration when making a decision where the safety and well-being of any individual or third parties is concerned.

6   When deciding on sharing information take into consideration what needs to be shared and to whom. An individual may not need to know everything but just what is relevant to them. Ensure that any information that is shared is also accurate, is done in a timely manner and the medium is secure.

7   Record any decisions you make about sharing or not sharing information. Make it clear what information was shared, to whom and the purpose of sharing that information.

(HM Government – Information Sharing Pocket Guide)

Information governance is a term you may have heard and not really understood. It is primarily concerned with the way an organisation deals with information. That is information generated, information received, information kept, information destroyed and so forth.

The HORUS Model To Information Handling

Held securely and confidential
Obtained fairly and efficiently
Recorded accurately and reliably
Used effectively and ethically
Shared appropriately and lawfully

Go to www.recordkeepingmadeeasybook.com to download a PDF with The Seven Golden Rules For Information Sharing and The HORUS Model To Information Handling.

Now that you understand the importance of record keeping are you ready to discover how to re-claim time to get more of it done, in Chapter 2.

Chapter 2

Write It Now And Save Time Later

Do you feel case recording takes up too much of your valuable time?

Do you relate to any of these statements?

- You hate paperwork and prefer the face to face work with service users.
- You're not sure about the level of detail expected in your case records and the best way to lay it out.
- You find electronic recording systems hard to read.
- You get frustrated when you have to cover for a colleague and their case records are unclear and difficult to understand.

In this chapter you will discover how to avoid writing poor case records, what information to put in, what information to leave out, and (how to) do it in less time.

Sonia Harris

How To Make Record Keeping a Priority

Do you find case recording tedious and boring? You enjoy working with the service users but you don't like being stuck at the computer recording what you have done. You find yourself putting off this task and then find that you have fallen so far behind that you struggle to get yourself up-to-date.

You are not alone. I've spoken to a number of practitioners who have started to worry about the amount of time they spend in front of the computer. In the Social Services Inspectorate report Recording with Care: inspection of case recording in social services department 1999, a social worker said:

"I didn't become a social worker because I wanted to be a typist or a computer programmer. I want to work with people, not waste my time in front of a machine." (Social Services Inspectorate, 1999)

People were complaining back in 1999 but now there is even more work that is computer based as organisations are moving towards being paperless.

You may even agree with the comment of another social worker:

"Recording is regarded by most practitioners as a necessary evil. It is resented as a distraction from the real work. In one inquiry after another, recording has been identified as an area of concern... Practitioners complain about the amount of paperwork that increasingly dominates the job, about cumbersome and unreliable electronic recording systems, and that recording is seen essentially as an administrative task and back-(side) covering exercise." (O'Rourke, 2009)

We all have tasks that we dislike, and even hate. It could be housework, washing the car, or filing, but whatever it is we will often do our best to avoid it. Case recording is no different and if it is a task that you hate you are more likely to procrastinate. If you don't wash the car the worst that will happen is it gets dirtier and dirtier. If you fail to keep your records up to date there may be missing information that can have adverse consequences.

What happens when you put off your case recording?

- When you keep information in your head and delay recording, key information may be forgotten.
- An accumulation in recording of complex cases could result in an insurmountable accumulation of paperwork that you cannot get on top of.
- A case inquiry could find that a lack of recording contributed to poor management of the case.

Even if you don't find record keeping tedious, you may find it difficult to prioritise your case recording:

- You prefer face to face work because you consider yourself a people person. It is important to have good interpersonal skills and be able to relate to the service users you work with. It is equally important that the work you do is written down so that at a future date you can review what has happened. It is also important for your colleagues and other professionals to see the work you have done and understand why you did what you did.

- Writing about what you have done is boring. Some people find writing a tedious task and will avoid it, but in the end this work has to be done. If it is rushed, it is more likely to have mistakes. If you avoid this important task, it builds up and in the end the job is much bigger than it was at the start. It is even more tedious if you have to write up several case records in one sitting rather than a single case record as you go along.

- During the normal working day you deal with continuous disturbances and distractions such as telephone calls or email messages. They may not be important but seem urgent because it is either the telephone ringing or an alert flashing. Then there is dealing with those drop-in visitors.

When a colleague drops by your desk for a quick chat, very rarely is it a short discussion. You don't want to appear rude, so you engage in conversation and before you know it, twenty minutes have passed. Remember, when time is spent, it cannot be reimbursed.

You perceive these interruptions as urgent because you hear the telephone ringing or see an email alert flashing.

Here Are Three Ways to Ensure You Prioritise Your Case Recording

1. **Recognise that case recording is an integral and essential part of your day to day practice.** You may not like it as a task but if you see it as important as other probation tasks you will give it the priority it deserves.

2. **Schedule time to record and keep to it.** It is easier to undertake a task that you dislike if you know when you will do it. Think about the part of the day that you are most productive. Is it mid or late morning or mid or late afternoon?

3. **Chain it to another task that you know will get done.** When you make an appointment with a service user you know that the meeting will take place, unless of course they do not turn up. A chain is made up of links connected to each

other. Decide to always create a link between an appointment and recording that meeting. There isn't one without the other. In your diary schedule the two tasks at the same time.

How to Banish Your Time Stealers

When they think of time management, most people believe it is just prioritising and keeping a to-do list. This is true to some extent, but it's more than meets the eye. Do you feel that everything is a priority? You feel you should set up systems but you just don't have the time?

Time management is more about managing you and your behaviour than managing time. The telephone rings. You want to ignore it but the ringing sounds urgent so you pick it up. It is a colleague wanting information about a service user you supervised a few years ago. She has a report to write and wants the information as soon as possible.

You go ahead and retrieve the information for her. At the end of the call you find out she wants the information now because she is on leave from tomorrow. The report she needs to write is not needed for another two weeks. You realise the call took 20 minutes. 20 minutes you will never get back for your own work. This shows you the important but not urgent rule. You can learn more about the time management matrix which explains how to prioritise urgent and important in his book The 7 Habits of Highly Effective People.

7 Time Stealers and How to Avoid Them

1. **Are you trying to get too much done in too little time?** You know that you have too much work to do but feel helpless about doing anything about it. The truth is you can't fit 10 hours of work into 7 hours. You don't get all the work done. The quality suffers and you end up with no sense of accomplishment.

Solutions:
- You know how much work you can handle. When you are given more work, show your manager your schedule. Let them decide what work needs to be prioritised and what work is put to one side.
- Plan at least a week's work in advance.
- The night before, write down 5 things you want to get done the next day, in order of priority. During the night your mind will start to work on it. The next morning get started on your most important task. Once you finish that task move on to the next. Whatever tasks you don't get done, put at the beginning of your list of 5 for the next day. Overestimate the amount of time you need to complete a piece of work.

2. **Are you prepared for a crisis?** Do you have to drop everything in an emergency? Imagine this scenario. Your morning is full of appointments with service users. You set time aside this afternoon to finish an important report that your manager expects tomorrow. You receive a message on your mobile phone. Your son has taken ill and the school want you to pick him up straight away. You have no choice you have to leave now. Your colleagues may be able to cover the appointments but what about that report?

Solutions:

- Anticipate crisis and plan the action that is needed to deal with it.

- You cannot plan for every crisis but there are ways of working that can reduce your stress. For example, if you have a deadline to complete a report why not artificially bring that deadline forward. This creates a buffer so that if there is an emergency you have given yourself a few extra days to get the work done.

3. **Are you continuously disturbed by the telephone?** You are in the flow and focused on completing a case record. The telephone rings; you pick it up and deal with the query. You return to your work but before you can get started again the telephone rings. This time the caller was put through in error by the receptionist. By the time you settle back into your work

a second time you are told your next appointment has arrived.

A telephone call can be urgent and important. It can also be not urgent and not important. You are tempted to answer the call because the ringing sounds urgent. Even a mobile with a silent facility vibrates or flashes the message "incoming call" that you find difficult to resist.

Solutions:
- Tell reception you will take calls at a specific time.
- Decide to respond to telephone calls at a specified time. For example, a half hour block at the end of the day may work.
- Record a voicemail. Inform your callers of the best time to call. Of if you prefer email, ask them to email you. Remember to clearly state and spell the email address you want them to use.
- When you take a call, politely let the caller know your time constraints at the start of the call. Announce that you have 10 minutes to talk.
- Avoid prolonged small talk at the start of a call. After the hello, ask "How may I help you today?"

4. **Is your inbox overloaded with email?** Do you dread taking time off because you know that an avalanche of emails will await you on your return?

Your manager, colleagues and external professionals use email as their primary communication. You have an email alert system set up so you check your emails as they drop into your inbox. This is a constant distraction from the other work you need to do.

Solutions:

- Attempt to handle an email only once and respond immediately. Delete emails that have been actioned or that require no action.
- Turn off the email alert. Schedule specific times during the day to check your emails.
- Create 3 email folders: Action, Hold and Archive. If the action will take more than a couple of minutes, file in the Action folder. The Hold folder is for temporary emails that contain information that you need easy access to or you are waiting for follow- up information. Your Archive folder will hold longer-term information. Sub-divide into subject and topic areas.
- Schedule time to deal with those emails that require more of your time to deal with.

(More about emails in chapter 7)

5. **Do drop-in visitors outstay their welcome?** A colleague stops at your desk and asks "Have you got a moment?" You are in the middle of an important report but your response is "Yes". You don't want to appear rude, so you engage in

conversation. After 20 minutes your colleague says "Gosh I can't continue our conversation. I set aside the next hour to finish an important piece of work. We'll catch up later." One person's break time is another person's work time.

Solutions:

- Don't be tempted to use this interruption as a useful distraction to take you away from a task that you do not like.
- Stand up. This should discourage the visitor from sitting down and will also give the message that you are busy.
- Don't engage in small talk. Find out quickly the nature of the query and if urgent and important deal with it immediately. If the matter is not urgent, schedule a more convenient time to discuss in more detail.

6. **Do you have a cluttered desk?** If you multi-task your desk can quickly become covered with paperwork. You can waste time looking for papers that have got mixed up. Paperwork can be misplaced in case files and then misfiled.

Solution:

- Have trays for incoming and outgoing mail.
- Have a tray for case files you work on during that day. Take out and work on one case file at a time. Put it back in the tray if you have to work on another case file.

- Create a space in a locked cupboard to place these trays at the end of the day.

7. **Do you procrastinate?** Do you put off tasks that you don't like? Unfortunately, when you put off a task it does not go away. In fact it grows until you can't put if off anymore. When you put off a task for too long it becomes too big to handle. If your case records are written on a note pad in a locked drawer they can't be accessed by your colleagues.

Solution:
- Schedule set times each day to complete tedious or repetitive tasks.
- Don't be tempted to put off tasks you don't like. Do them at the time you scheduled.
- If it is a large task break it up into small chunks that are easier to handle.

Now that you have learnt how to take back control of your time and environment, are you ready to find out how to use critical thinking skill and make your records more readable in Chapter 3?

Chapter 3

What To Put In And What To Leave Out

In the last chapter you learnt some strategies to prioritise record keeping and banish time stealers.

Is this scenario familiar?

This has been one of those days when you have seen one service user after the other, with no time in between to write up the sessions. You are in a rush and you write down what you believe is enough to give a gist of what is happening. You tell yourself that you will add more details tomorrow when you have more time. Of course when tomorrow comes, you're onto a new crisis and you do not add to the record.

The more time that elapses between the event and recording it, the more likely it is that you will forget certain details. Should you suddenly go off sick, a colleague picking up your case will not have access to the information in your head.

In this chapter you will learn some ideas to help you understand the importance of writing concise records that include accurate information and make them easier to read.

So how detailed does a case record need to be to convey enough information so that someone else looking at the case knows exactly what is going on? Your records should include the following 4 key principles:

1. Must include critical information
2. Must be clear and easy to read
3. Critical information can be found quickly
4. Clear distinction between fact and opinion

Importance of Distinguishing Fact From Opinion

A lot of time can be wasted if you do not make a clear distinction between what is fact and what is your opinion. Getting this wrong can lead to misinformation and even service user complaints. In situations where you have to make hasty judgements about risk it is important to be able to quickly distinguish between information that is factual and those based on opinion.

The consequences of using fact and opinion interchangeably can be serious. A service user could be refused help if you have incorrectly recorded information as fact. You must be able to back up a fact with evidence. You cannot take everything you read or hear at face value.

Critical thinking skills will help you to evaluate information and distinguish fact from opinion. You will be able to determine whether or not information you read or hear is genuine. You will be able to distinguish between primary and secondary sources of information.

Consider this scenario:

You receive a telephone call from a colleague. She tells you that your client, John, was seen driving yesterday. She is telling you this because she knows John is banned from driving. You saw John earlier today and he was adamant that he's not driven since committing the offence of drink driving. This is disappointing because you thought he was making good progress. He has two previous convictions for driving whilst disqualified. You need to record this information.

You record the following:

"John was seen driving yesterday. When I saw John earlier today he was obviously lying about not driving since his offence. He just can't keep away from cars. He has had at least 2 previous driving bans and I can't see the situation

changing. I will give him a piece of my mind when he comes in for his next appointment."

Let's break down each section and consider whether the information recorded is fact or opinion.

John was seen driving yesterday.
- The information is stated as fact.
- We don't know who saw John driving
- Can we trust the source of the information?
- The information has not been verified.
- We don't know where John was seen driving

When I saw John earlier today he was obviously lying about not driving since his offence.
- Assumption has been made that John is lying.
- Information is being treated as if it is fact without verification.
- It is subjective

He just can't keep away from cars.
- A judgement is being made here although information has not been verified
- Assumption being made that this is ongoing
- Is previous history enough to make this judgement now?

He has had at least 2 previous driving bans and I can't see the situation changing.

- Previous convictions are fact.
- "I can't see the situation changing" is subjective and biased.

You may have picked up more issues but I think you get the point.

Here Is The same Record Rewritten With The Principles of Critical Thinking

Record of a short telephone conversation I had with Jane Smith, Probation Officer based at Another Probation Office, Tel: 0123 456 7890. I was unable to obtain full information because the telephone call was cut short because Jane had an emergency to deal with.

Jane told me John Smith was seen driving yesterday. This is third party information. I need further information about who saw the service user driving, when and where. At this moment I cannot confirm this information is fact. If this information is from another service user I must check that it is not malicious. John reported to me this morning and gave no indication that he had been driving.

Plan

1. *I will call Jane Smith tomorrow, 25/08/15 at 10 am to find out source of information and whether it can be verified. This information will not be disclosed to John before verification of source of the information.*

2. *If information is verified by a reliable source I will talk to John on 31/08/15, his next scheduled appointment, about driving whilst on a ban and the consequences should he be arrested.*

Importance Of Including Relevant Information

It is important to keep records succinct and to the point. However, this is sometimes taken to the extreme and critical information is left out.

What do You Think About This Case Record?

"John telephoned and said he would be able to make the appointment tomorrow with Stephen."

What is wrong with this record?

- We have no idea who John or Stephen is.
- Stephen or John may be the service user and their name would be on the record; however, what if the third party has

the same first name as the service user?

- If John or Stephen is a professional, we do not have their title, the organisation they represent or a contact number.
- We don't have any information about what the appointment is about, when it is (date), or where it is to be held.
- We don't know who took the call.
- If the case holder took the call, what if they were suddenly taken ill? Would their colleague know who to contact?
- Date and time of tomorrow's meeting is missing.
- If the receptionist took the call, they have assumed that the case holder has all the details.

Here is what the same record looks like rewritten with additional information

John Smith, Project worker, Backontrack Hostel, (tel-xxx xxxx xxxx) telephoned today, 20 August 2015 at 9:15 am to confirm that he would be attending the three way meeting with me (Offender Manager) and Stephen tomorrow 21 August 2015 from 2:30 pm to 3:30 pm at the Probation Office.

Let's break down each section to see what makes it a better record

John Smith, **(first and second name makes the individual more identifiable)** *Project worker,* **(John's title tells us that he** *is a professional) Backontrack Hostel, (know the organisation that John represents) (tel-xxx xxxx xxxx)(telephone number gives a means of contacting John if further information is required or the appointment needed to be cancelled or postponed) (telephoned today, 20 August 2015 at 9:15 am (we know the exact date and time the call was taken which if helps information needs to verified)* to confirm that he would be attending the three way meeting with me *(Offender Manager)(we know who took the telephone call)* and Stephen tomorrow 21 August 2015 from 2:30 pm to 3:30 pm *(date and time recorded clearly)* at the Probation Office *(venue for the meeting clearly recorded).*

This record involves a bit more work and more time. However, there are a number of benefits to recording in this way. If a colleague was to review this information in the absence of the case holder, they have all the information about the third party professional. They would be able to make contact immediately if the meeting needed to be rearranged. We know what the appointment is about, when and where it is going to happen. We also know how long the appointment is scheduled for. We know that the record has been written by the person responsible for the case.

What about readability of case records?

Do you proofread all your case records? If someone else had to read what you had written would they understand what you were trying to say? If you don't have time to proofread all your case records it is likely that there will be some overlooked spelling mistakes and grammatical errors. Most records are produced electronically and so we don't have the problem of trying to decipher someone else's. We assume that as professional practitioners we have a good understanding of the English language.

Do you relate to any of the following?

- I don't think spelling, long sentences and the odd typo is important; it is the content that matters.
- I have read some case records with grammatical errors that give an ambiguous meaning.
- Everyone uses abbreviations, acronyms and jargon; I've just copied what everyone else does.
- Other departments use abbreviations that I am not familiar with and if the original word is not in a previous record I have had to ring up that department to find out what it means.
- I am dyslexic and I sometimes find it difficult to understand my colleagues' records.

Have you seen records that suffer from the following?

- Information is repeated.
- Lack focus.
- Include typos.
- Information is not in chronological order.
- Narrative rather than analytical.
- Similar information is written in different places.
- New information is tagged onto the end and not appropriately linked to information written earlier in the record.

When a record is difficult to read it causes the following problems:

- Easily misunderstood.
- Information is misinterpreted.
- Colleagues waste time trying to decipher the message. The author may also struggle to understand what they have written when reviewing it in the future.
- Colleagues will take up your time asking you to explain what you have written.

Ultimately, information that is misunderstood could lead to complaints from service users. You must also consider colleagues and service users who may have a communication problem like dyslexia, a learning disability. They may have difficulty reading text with abbreviations, long paragraphs and sentences.

10 ways to Make your Case Records Easier to Read

1. **Know Your Audience.** Who is going to read and review your records? Keep that in mind as you pick your writing style. What information will they need to find? Get to the point and make sure everything is clear. Remember that service users can ask to see your records.

   At a minimum, record the time and date of contact, what occurred, and next steps to take. Use a method that is universal so that you are in compliance with your organisation. You want your record keeping to pass any auditing exercise too.

2. **Keep It Simple.** Don't write in a manner that tries to impress. Use language that is common and that makes sense. Good grammar and punctuation is important. Stick to the facts too. If you have an opinion, state it as such.

   Colleagues in your probation department rely on your details. Make sure there is no risk of misinterpretation.

3. **Use Bold Headings.** The use of headings is a great way to break up the sections in your writing. As a probation practitioner, you want to be able to easily refer back to what you have documented.

You also want to make it as simple as possible for others to identify certain information quickly.

There are times when your colleagues need to read small segments of what you have completed. Headings prevent them from wasting time reading everything.

4. **Use Paragraphs.** As a probation practitioner, the last thing you want is lines and lines of text that go on endlessly. This is why paragraph use is so important.

It helps to identify the information in a way that is appealing. Combined with headings, the use of paragraphs really does offer a professional appearance in record keeping.

5. **Use Short paragraphs.** Don't let all of the writing run on and on. Break it up into paragraphs that are short and to the point. This is going to be easy on the eyes and it makes scanning for details so much easier for the reader.

Well-organised record keeping also looks professional to others who rely on that information. You will appreciate it too when you go back and read what you have documented later on.

6. **Use short sentences.** Correct grammar is very important in your records, so use short sentences. However, you don't want to have fragmented sentences.

If you have a sentence that is too long, the meaning can get lost. Write in short sentences just like you would if you were talking to someone.

Try to avoid going over 17 words in a sentence. Stick to only one idea in any given sentence.

7. **Abbreviations.** While you may be tempted to abbreviate, don't do it. It may take you less time to read but think about the reader. It will take a reader much longer to read an abbreviated term they are not familiar with.

However, there are times when you can abbreviate long terms that are very common within your organisation. Write the term in full the first time and then use the abbreviation for the rest of the record. Ask your manager about an approved list of abbreviations that can be used in your role.

8. **Acronyms.** Acronyms should be used sparingly in record keeping. When you use an acronym, put the meaning of it in brackets so that it can be identified quickly by a reader who may not recognise it.

9. **Spell Check.** You can catch plenty of spelling and grammar errors with spell check. However, that shouldn't be your only means of proofing what you have recorded.

   Use a dictionary to help you with complex spelling issues. You want to appear professional and spelling mistakes will stand out like a sore thumb.

10. **Proofread.** Spell checker may not always pick up a wrong word. Make sure sentences are complete and not too long.

    Read through your information before you submit it. Reading it out aloud makes it easier to pick up mistakes.

    Does the information you wrote make sense? Do you have all of the details? Is the information accurate?

    For example, if a client isn't showing up for appointments that should be documented too.

I have created a short ebook "10 Steps To Faster, Easy To Write Record Keeping For Probation Practitioners." You can download the ebook by visiting the official website for this book: www.recordkeepingmadeeasybook.com **

Now that you understand how to use critical thinking skills and make your records more readable, in Chapter 4 I'm going to share an example of a structured layout that will speed up your record keeping.

Chapter 4

Sonia's PAP™ Record Keeping System For Probation Practitioners

Do you know how to present your information so that it is easy to pick out information you need quickly? Some people write in a narrative style. They tell a story that includes everything that happened in the session from start to finish. If you write in this style, how easy is it to find specific information? Do you find yourself saying "I know I wrote it in here somewhere but where is it?" How much time do you waste scanning through a record to find one piece of information?

In this chapter I share with you a record keeping format that you can use to record information so that you:

- Know exactly where to put certain information.
- Reduce the time wasted thinking about how to present information.
- Make it easier for you find the information you need.
- Make it easier to add information in the right place at a later date.

The medical and therapeutic professions use the SOAP (Subjective, Observation, Assessment and Plan) and DAP (Data, Assessment and Plan) recording systems to ensure a consistent approach to case recording of patient contacts. I have used these two approaches to come up with a version that may be helpful to probation practitioners.

The Purpose Assessment Plan™ (PAP™) Record Keeping System for Probation Practitioners

Purpose - of session/record/telephone call/email
Clearly state why the contact took place

Supervision session with service user
- What was planned for today's session?
- Were there any issues from last time that need to be covered today?
- Were there any concerns about risk that need to be followed up today?
- If the session did not go to plan then give an explanation.

Telephone call or Email
- State who telephoned or sent the email.
- State reason for the telephone call or email.
- Summary of what was said during telephone call or written in email.

- Record the main issues discussed/covered.
- Record any requests made with time scales if relevant.
- If confidential information was shared record reason and confirm you adhered to information sharing protocols.

Assessment/Analysis

What happened in the session/meeting?

What was content of telephone call/email?

Supervision session with service user

- What happened in the session?
- What was the intervention/focus of session related to sentence plan objectives (if appropriate)? Use headings.
- What did the service user say?
- Did the service user participate/do what you wanted them to do?
- Give your judgement of the current level of risk. Has it increased or decreased? Provide evidence for your judgement, state the action you will take and who you will communicate with.
- State any significant event or series of events. Review and update OASys.
- State your observations of the service user's mood and appearance. Use words such as "appeared," "seemed" or "as evidenced by."

- State your professional judgement about the service user's issues/problems

You are not expected to record all of the above in a single case record. This is to give you an idea of the type of information you could record after meeting with a service user.

Plan

What will happen after the session/meeting/telephone call/email? What is the next action?

Supervision session with service user

- State the date and time the service user needs to report to you again. Record if given verbally and or in writing. Any written instruction should be photocopied.
- If there are any issues or problems to address state what you plan to do next.
- If you have actions for the service user state what you asked them to do, how and by when.
- If homework is given to the service user. State what it is, the format and timescale for completion.
- If a referral is needed. State the service provider, purpose, when the referral will be made, named person to be contacted or contact details.
- State the plan for the next session.

Telephone call or email

- Action to be taken by you with time scale.
- Action to be taken by other person with time scale.
- Following a telephone call consider if it is appropriate send a follow up email to confirm content of discussion and actions to be taken.

Example of a Case Record Using the PAP™ Record Keeping System

Brief Background to the Case

David Smith was sentenced to a Community Order with a requirement to attend for alcohol treatment by the courts for an offence of assault. He reports to probation every week and is also required to see an alcohol counsellor on a weekly basis. He has a previous conviction for an assault against a previous partner. He has been in his current relationship for 3 months.

Case Record

Purpose of session

This is a scheduled session with David. Offender Manager will discuss progress with addressing alcohol issues and sessions with counsellor. Request update on current situation with his relationship.

Assessment/Analysis

David attended for his scheduled supervision meeting.

Alcohol – David is scheduled to see the alcohol counsellor every Tuesday morning. He did not attend appointment this morning. He told me he was hung over. Today is the second appointment he has missed with the alcohol counsellor. He disclosed that his drinking had increased over the weekend and he was worried about a total relapse. This is the second week David has come into the office smelling of alcohol and he appears to be struggling to maintain abstinence.

David was visibly shaking during the session. I could smell stale alcohol on his breath. His appearance was unkempt and he seemed very worried about his drinking. He became very defensive and agitated when talking about what triggered his drinking. He was reluctant to disclose his drinking levels.

An increase in drinking could suggest an increase in risk. He offends when he is under the influence of alcohol. His request for help suggests he is beginning to accept he has a problem.

During the session I telephoned John Brown, alcohol counsellor, New Direction, (01234 567 890) and a new appointment was offered for tomorrow (17/03/13) at 2:30 pm.

Relationships – David said, "Me and Sarah have been arguing. I don't want to go back to my old ways; otherwise she will leave me again." He said that there was no violence. I am concerned about any possible domestic abuse against his partner, as he assaulted a previous partner.

Plan

David was given instructions to report to me on Tuesday 14th August 2013 at 12:30 pm. David given written appointment with the alcohol counsellor tomorrow, 17/03/13 at 2:30 pm. He was told that if he did not attend he would be in breach of his order. Copy of appointment taken and placed on file.

I will contact police today to find out if there have been any police call outs to David's address.

I will call John Brown, alcohol counsellor, New Direction, Tel: 01234 567 890 to confirm that David attended and find out his assessment and plan.

The next session will review progress regarding alcohol and discuss relationship issues.

I will review OASys and SARA and if I believe there has been a significant increase in risk of harm I will discuss with my line manager.

Now that you have seen an example of how to structure your case record using the PAP™ Record Keeping System, in Chapter 5 we will look at how you can get the right balance between work, family and your personal interests.

Chapter 5

Get More Done At Work And Enjoy Your Life At Home

Do you get in early in the morning and leave late each day? You do this extra time but you still can't get on top of your work. Then you worry about taking time off. You work twice as hard because you don't want to leave your colleagues in the lurch. You have even been known to cancel leave or return early. When you return you work twice as hard again to catch up. You feel tired and unwell because you haven't really had a break. You worry about taking time off sick and the cycle starts all over again. Is this familiar?

Heavy workloads, tight deadlines, together with threatened job security, all add to the pressure of working longer hours and taking fewer breaks. Practitioners want to provide a high quality service to their clients during times when staffing is low. They feel guilty if they take time out because they know their colleagues have to take up any slack.

In this chapter you will learn how you can take control of your time at work so that you can be more present, and enjoy life with your family when you're away from the office.

Here are three things that can happen if you don't get your work-life balance right:

- You are less productive.
- You are less able to manage stress.
- You have less time for your family and yourself outside of work.

You might be the one that is getting in the way of having the right balance between work, family and your personal interests. If you understand the mistake you might be making, you will be able to put the balance back into your life.

5 Work Life Balance Mistakes and what you can do about them to help you feel happier and less distracted

1. You Don't Take Regular Time Out

Not taking your holiday leave entitlement could be damaging your health. You need to take time out to recharge your batteries. Working long hours without regular breaks means you are more likely to make fatigue-related mistakes. Poor performance could put you at risk of losing your job when it might be a case that you are too tired.

Here are 4 things you can do to make sure you take your holiday:

* Make sure you know how much annual leave entitlement you have.
* Plan your holiday leave in advance and book it in with your manager in good time. Schedule it so that you take some leave during each quarter of the year.
* Leave space in your schedule prior to your leave to deal with any last minute emergencies.
* Don't be tempted to schedule lots of appointments during your first week back from leave. Leave space to deal with any urgent issues that came up whilst you were away.

2. You Don't Plan Time to Rest, Exercise and Nourish Yourself

Do you take a lunch break? Do you take 5 minutes to eat a sandwich at your desk and then get straight back to work? Do you skip lunch altogether to shorten your day at the office? Do you use your lunch to catch up on personal admin? You may think that you are getting more done or that you are giving yourself more time at the end of the day. The truth is, by the end of the day you probably feel so beat down that you don't feel like doing anything else.

It is important to take some time out during the day. It is an opportunity for you to refresh yourself so that you feel more motivated to focus on the rest of the day. Even a 15 minute break will give you the time to unwind and distract from the pressures of work. At the end of the working day you may even have the energy to go to the gym or to see that film you have been promising yourself.

Here are 5 examples of things you can do to unwind and refresh during your working day:

- If you are not used to taking a lunch break start scheduling a lunch break of at least 15 to 20 minutes. It is less likely to be hijacked if you have locked it into your diary. Grab a colleague to share lunch with.
- Remember to eat and drink water. Choose something healthy. Cook an extra portion the night before to bring in for lunch the next day. Always have a glass of water on your desk that you refill throughout the day.
- Meditation, yoga, breathing.
- Power Nap. No more than 20 to 30 minutes.
- Exercise. You need a longer lunch break but you could fit in a 20 minute walk.

It is not easy taking time out for yourself, but the consequence of not doing so is a buildup of stress, and eventually this affects your health. If you would like some help to deal with your stress, visit www.recordkeepingmadeeasybook.com and register for my "Stamp Out Destructive Stress: A 7 Part Stress Management e-Course For Probation Practitioners.

3. You Don't Negotiate Flexibility

Are you a working parent struggling to balance the demands of work and doing the school run? Are you part of the sandwich generation, juggling grandparent responsibilities with caring for ageing parents? Are you approaching retirement and wanting more time to enjoy new personal interests? Is your commute to work leaving you stressed and tired before you even start? Flexible working hours may be the solution to you having the work-life balance that has been eluding you.

There is already UK legislation for parents and guardians to request flexible working if they have a dependent child or relative. You might think that this is not open to you because you are not in this situation. The legislation only gives the right to ask, it does not assume you will have that request accepted.

Whether or not you believe your employer will be responsive to a request for flexible working, if you don't ask you will never know. A flexible working arrangement could be one of the following:

- Later start and finish or earlier start and finish.
- Flexible leave arrangements to fit in with school holidays.
- Working longer and shorter weeks interchangeably.
- Combination of shorter and longer days during the week
- Part time working.
- Job sharing.
- Working from a different location.
- Working from home.

Here are things to do before approaching your employer with a request for flexible working:

- Make sure you already have a reputation within your organisation of being a valuable and dependable member of staff.
- Talk to colleagues about what you want to do. You might find someone else who wants to change their working hours. You could put in a joint plan.
- Talk to colleagues who have already successfully requested flexible working. Find out what case they put forward.
- If you belong to a union, speak to a rep first before approaching your employer. The rep may be able to give you some advice and guidance about putting a plan together.

- Devise a plan that focuses on two key areas. Firstly, how the change will positively impact on the business, that is, improve performance. Secondly, how you will minimise any potential negative impact, for example, workload. Does the plan meet both the employer's and your needs? Be clear about the reasons why you want to change and the solutions. Show how the new working arrangement could be trialled. This is your starting point for negotiation so be willing to be flexible.

- Be willing to give something up. To accommodate your request you may need to work fewer hours and so receive less pay. This may be worth it because what you gain will be of greater value.

4. You Feel Guilty when you don't get everything done

Do you try to do everything yourself? Do you believe that if you stop, everything around you will fall apart? What about the expectations you set for yourself? Do you feel guilty when you can't achieve everything? If you are not careful you could be heading for burn-out.

There is only so much you can do in any given time. Working at a frantic pace so that you can fit it all in does not necessarily mean you do more. It can work against you because your manager may believe that you can manage the workload when the opposite is true. You not only want to get the job done, you want it to be perfect. And not only do you want it perfect at work, you expect it in your home life too. Aren't you setting yourself up? It is not possible to get things right all the time because sometimes we mess up.

What do you do when you can't get it all done and you don't get something right? You beat yourself up and feel guilty. Have you heard of the saying "Guilt is a wasted emotion?" You can also get fearful about people thinking you are not competent. The problem with both guild and fear is that you end up putting in more hours to prove you can get the work done.

Here are some ways to help you avoid the trap of thinking you can get it done and get it right all of the time:

- Don't set yourself unreasonably high expectations.
- Accept that you can't get everything done. Use time management strategies to prioritise and manage your time.
- Ask for help. Share the load.
- Change your perspective about making mistakes. Don't see mistakes as failures. See mistakes as an opportunity to learn and grow.
- Stop beating yourself up when you don't get things done.

5. You Don't Pay Enough Attention to Your Home Life and Relationships

Are you preoccupied with work when you are at home? Do you feel guilty about not spending enough time with your children, and so you overindulge them? You may hate missing out on time with your partner or children because you work late or bring work home. Even when you have time with your family, you may feel too stressed out to enjoy it.

Here are 3 simple steps to free up time to spend with your family even if you are busy and overworked:

1. Make a list of your goals in life. This list could include spending time with your family, reading, going to the cinema, exercise. You can make this a family activity so everyone has a chance to add the things they want to do. Just as you would prioritise tasks at work, prioritise a short list of things you want to do both individually and as a family.

2. Create space in your life by getting rid of other things on your schedule. What don't you have to do? Are there things you can delegate? Do you spend a lot of time watching TV or surfing the internet as a form of distraction?

3. It is only when you have created space that you can make dates with your family to do the things you have prioritised. Lock those dates into your diary and make them sacred. The last thing you want is to not turn up because it wasn't written down and you scheduled in something else. Have a date night with your partner at the weekend. If you have more than one child, schedule a date with each one every week to do an activity that they like. Schedule family time each week doing an activity that you all like and that is fun. The "date" can be as little as 20 minutes; what matters is that it is quality time without distractions.

Now that you have some ideas on how to take control of your time so that you have more time for you and your family, you are ready to find out how to get to grips with the new world of information technology in Chapter 6.

Chapter 6

How To Be Tech Savvy

Are you fed up with the computer system freezing or crashing just before an important deadline? Have you ever lost a document and spent ages looking for it, only to have to start it all over again? How many times have you sent an email and forgotten to add the attachment? These may seem like minor problems but they can lead to major irritations when valuable time is lost.

In this chapter you will be given tips and tricks to eradicate some of those computer frustrations. I will also share some shortcuts to give you a better computer experience.

Handling computer stress and frustration

As most of your work is computer based there is very little you can do when the computer system goes down. The biggest fear is that the computer crashes right in the middle of typing a report. When the system is back up you realise that the last paragraph you typed was not saved. Not only have you lost time because the computer was out of action, you now have to remember what you originally typed.

It is not surprising that you feel angry and frustrated when your computer stops cooperating. You may not have control over how the computers work, but you can decide how you will respond.

4 Tips on Handling Computer Stress

1. **Be prepared.** You know that from time to time the computer system will freeze or crash. Have the attitude that this is outside of your control and there isn't anything you can do about it.

2. **Make your work environment safe.** Firstly, make sure that any required adjustments are made to your work station to ensure it is ergonomically safe. Your posture and the way you sit at your computer can affect how you feel and function. A build-up of tension in your body may have a negative impact on how you respond to minor frustrations. There are simple relaxation techniques that you can do whilst sitting at your desk. Remember to take a break at least every hour or two. Take a short walk.

There is a module on posture in my "Stamp Out Destructive Stress: A 7 Part Stress Management e-Course For Probation Practitioners" **at** www.recordkeepingmadeeasybook.com

3. **Get up and walk away.** If there isn't other work you can do in the meantime, stop and take a break. Your colleagues will be in the same boat so take the opportunity to have some downtime.

4. **Save your work regularly.** If you use Microsoft Word it has an auto save facility. You can adjust it so that it saves more frequently, say every minute. When you reopen your document only the last minute of your work will be unsaved.

Turbo Charge Your Computer Literacy Skills

Maybe you don't see yourself as particularly computer savvy. Even if you are confident about your computer skills there may still be some issues that slow your progress. Has this happened to you?

- You lose the flow in your typing because you constantly need to use the mouse.
- You had to sit at another computer workstation and struggled to use the ergonomic mouse.

- You accidently deleted a document without thinking and thought it was lost forever.
- You are sure you saved that document but you can't find it anywhere.
- You accidently highlighted a passage as you typed a letter and the sentence disappeared.
- You accidently click "no" when asked if you want to save a document.
- 5 minutes after sending an email the recipient replies asking for the attachment.

You probably view these as minor irritations and just put up with them. Imagine these happening several times in a day. Over a week and a month the time lost soon adds up. It is important to practice good computer habits and learn some useful tricks and short cuts.

5 Tips And Tricks To Eradicate Minor Tech Frustrations

1. You accidently highlight a sentence when you type a letter and the passage disappears.

   Fix: Immediately go to Edit and click on Undo.

2. You accidently delete your document.

   Fix: Go to the Recycle Bin and look for your work. When found click on it and accept recover option.

3. You click on "No" accidently when asked if you want to save document.

   Fix: Change your auto save to every minute. Your document will automatically save changes made in the last minute.

4. You saved the document but you can't find it.

   Fix: Check the temporary files. Do advanced search.

5. You forgot to add the email attachment again

   Fix: Attach document to the email before you start writing the content of your email.

Tired of Chasing Your Mouse?

Did you know your computer can be entirely operated by your keyboard? Ditching the mouse could mean typing is both faster and easier.

Common Keyboard Shortcuts in Windows/
Top 12 Keyboard Shortcuts

1. **F1** - Displays the help file for the current program.
2. **F3** – Search for a file or folder
3. **Alt + f** - ' File '
4. **Ctrl + z** - Undo the last action.
5. **Ctrl + y** – redo
6. **Ctrl + a** – select all
7. **Ctrl + x** – Cuts selected text\graphics to the clipboard.
8. **Ctrl + s** – save
9. **Ctrl + p** - print
10. **Alt + Tab** - Quickly switch between current running programs.
11. **Ctrl + c** - Copies selected text\graphics to the clipboard.
12. **Ctrl + v** - Pastes text\graphics from the clipboard.

You can download a handy PDF sheet with the 12 Keyboard Shortcuts to put by your computer. Just visit www.recordkeepingmadeeasybook.com to download a copy.

Touch Typing V Hunt and Peck

Many tasks that you do as a probation practitioner are done on computers, laptops or mobile devices such as tablets or mobile phones. Let me ask you a question. Did anyone teach you how to type? I'm guessing that you use the "hunt and peck" typing method. If you don't know what that is, let me give you the following description. You use two fingers, the index finger of each hand. You search the keyboard for the letter or character you want and hit it with one of your index fingers.

Now you may be one of the fortunate ones, who learnt to touch type. Or maybe you work next to someone who touch types. The main thing that distinguishes someone who touch types from someone who hunts and pecks is the speed. Touch typing is much faster than hunt and peck typing, and not just for obvious reasons. Or maybe those reasons are not so obvious.

5 Benefits of Touch Typing

1. Saves You Time

As a hunt and peck typist you constantly stop your typing to look at the keyboard. If you've ever watched a touch typist, they keep their eyes on the screen whilst their fingers automatically hit the correct keys. A hunt and peck typist may only reach a speed of around 30 words per minute. When you are able to keep your eyes on the screen it is amazing how fast your fingers can fly across the keys. A touch typist can achieve speeds of over 70 words per minute. This means you can complete a piece of work in half the time.

2. Better focus

When you hunt and peck, you take your eyes away from the screen and look at the keyboard. This action breaks your focus. The time your eyes are away from the screen may seem minimal but you constantly have to focus and refocus on two different things. Touch typing means better focus and better flow with your thoughts because you are not losing concentration from the text you're typing.

3. Increased accuracy

As a hunt and peck typist you are spelling each word as you watch your fingers hit each key. When you look up and find you've typed a word incorrectly you have to go through the same hunt and peck process again. Sometimes, of course, you will miss an error because you're not totally focussed on the words on the screen. Touch typists have their eyes on the screen most of the time. It is easy to pick up errors quickly and correct them using the back space. They don't even have to take their eyes off the screen.

4. Improve your health

Good posture is important to ensure you don't end up with back problems. A hunt and peck typist will continuously look down at the keyboard. That means their neck and back will be hunched over. A touch typist looks straight ahead at the screen, very rarely needing to look down at the keyboard.

5. Reduces fatigue

If you've been stuck typing for hours you'll know how mentally and physically exhausting it can be. A touch typist focuses on one thing, the screen. All ten fingers are in use and automatically remember where each key is. There is no additional mental energy needed in switching gaze from screen to keyboard. No need to watch two fingers search out the correct key. No brain power needed in spelling out each word a split second before the forefinger hits the key.

You've just had a crash course on handling computer stress, dealing with minor technical problems and learnt the benefits of touch typing. Now let's move onto the final chapter and see what we can do about taming your email inbox.

Chapter 7

Email – How to Tame Your Email Inbox

Have you been overwhelmed by the number of emails you have in your inbox when you return to work following a period of leave or sickness?

Do you leave emails festering unanswered in your inbox?

Are you suffering from email overload?

Do you feel compelled to check your email frequently throughout the day?

I think emails are a bit like a ringing telephone.

Imagine this situation; you are sitting at your desk and the telephone rings. You are in the middle of writing an important report and you really don't want to be distracted. For a split second you consider ignoring it and letting it go to voicemail but you give in because there is something about the ring of a telephone that is urgent. You pick up the telephone and the person at the other end of the call says "Oh Mary, sorry I thought I was calling Sarah. I am up to here with work, how is it going with you ....?" The conversation goes on for 5 to 10 minutes and when you get off the telephone it takes you a good 5 to 10 minutes to get back into your flow. You are also kicking yourself that you did not ignore the call in the first place.

Emails can be as intrusive as telephone calls. In this chapter you will be given top tips on email etiquette and how to have control over your email rather than it having control over you.

Email is now the primary medium for exchanging information. Emails have taken over from the telephone, letters and faxes. Information sent via email is in the other person's inbox within seconds. Unlike a telephone conversation it is an immediate written record. The same information can be disseminated to many people at the same time, with no need for repetition.

But ...there are so many things that can go wrong with emails. Sometimes emails that are meant to be formal can contain informal conversations. Once you hit the send button, that email is a permanent record and whatever has been recorded cannot be taken back.

It is important to remember that email exchanges are a formal record that could be seen by a service user or used in formal proceedings. It is "written" evidence of what you have said.

It is easier to misinterpret a conversation that takes place using email because, unlike a face to face or telephone conversation, the tonality is missing.

Have you ever received an email from someone and become angry because of how it was written? Did you respond immediately and then regret what you said after you hit the send button?

I had not really paid much attention to how I replied to emails until an incident where I accidently forwarded an email to the wrong person. I had received an email from someone and was not too happy with the content of the email. I decided to forward the email to my manager with a comment about the original email. Unfortunately, I did not realise I hit the reply button instead of the forward button. I noticed the mistake a split second after hitting the send button.

I could hear the scream in my head, "Oh Nooooo", and my heart jumped. I quickly reviewed what I had written in the email and thankfully I did not make any derogatory comments. I quickly followed up with an email apologising and stating that the email was sent in error. Luckily there was no fallout. However, since then I am extra careful when I am forwarding or replying to an email. I also now consider using the telephone instead of an email when I need to give sensitive feedback.

Here is a quick top tip, should you find yourself in this situation again. Write the email but instead of sending it immediately, save it to your drafts. Come back to it later, preferably the next day if it can wait that long. You are now in a better frame of mind to write the email without that original emotion.

Email is a great communication tool and I wouldn't want to go back to relying on the post and old style memorandums. So I researched the internet and found lots of top tips on email etiquette. I tried to condense this information into 10 Top Tips but there was so much that I thought would benefit you that I have shared most of it here.

18 Top Tips On How To Send Emails

1. Remember that an email is an official communication and the same rules apply as with other written communication such as a letter, memo or fax.

2. Ensure an email is the most appropriate medium for the message you want to send.

3. Think of an email as the electronic equivalent of a postcard. Anyone may have access to it along its passage.

4. Make sure the subject line is meaningful by making sure it clearly states what the subject matter is about. When responding to an email, make sure you change the subject line to reflect your message. A clear and informative subject line will help your recipient to prioritise and decide quickly whether it is worth opening the email.

5. Always use a salutation or greeting such as "Dear ..." or "Hello ..." depending on whether you know the person.

6. Try to focus on one topic per email. Keep it simple, succinct and to the point. Limit paragraphs to about 6 sentences and where your email contains multiple messages consider using sub-headings or numbering each paragraph. Remember to separate each paragraph with a blank line.

7. State clearly what you want. During a busy working day staff expect to receive a high number of emails. People do not want to be engaged in numerous messages going back and forth, they want to clear their inbox as quickly as possible so that they can get on to the next task.

8. Be professional and careful about what you say to people. Do not assume that your email will be kept confidential because it can be easily forwarded. Unlike face to face interactions, written information is without non-verbal gestures or tonality, so messages have the potential of being misinterpreted.

9. Use proper grammar and punctuation. Do not be tempted to use shortcuts or what is sometimes termed as "text speak". In the work setting emails should be viewed as official documents, and therefore require a formal approach. Be aware that the contents of an email could be used in legal proceedings.

10. Use plain language to limit the risk of the information being misinterpreted.

11. If you are frustrated, angry or upset, give yourself time to calm down before sending an email. Save the original as a draft, do another task and then come back to it. When you re-read it think about the language you have used and whether it is likely to inflame the situation.

12. Re-read your email and reflect on what you have written before sending it. Remember to treat emails as official documents, so proofread and use the spell checker even

though it may not pick up all your typing mistakes.

13. When sending an email to a large group of people, be sure that they all really need to receive it, put the email addresses in the bcc field and send to yourself. This is particularly important if the information is sensitive because the email addresses will be hidden. Additionally when the email group is very large the receivers don't have to scroll down several lines before they can read the message or end up with wasted paper if the message needs to be printed off.

14. If you are copying in a third party ensure they need to have the information and provide a reason why they are receiving the email.

15. Ensure your email signature contains the following information: your name, title, department, organisation, contact telephone number and mobile if appropriate.

16. Any emails that are written, sent, printed off, stored and even deleted will be subject to the FOI Act 2000 and / or the Data Protection Act 1998. The FOI Act means that the public will have a right to the information contained within the email. If an email contains information about an individual, the data subject, they will be covered by the Data Protection Act and have a right to see the information written about them.

17. If you have a file to attach to an email consider whether or not you can copy and paste the most important parts into the body of the email. This will avoid having large files which may be difficult to download.

18. When sending an email giving information only, consider adding "No reply needed".

14 Top Tips On How To Reply to Emails

1. Set time aside once or twice per day to deal with your emails. Consider waiting until late morning for your first review as this will allow you to complete some of those tasks that you were not able to complete yesterday. Review your emails again an hour before the end of your working day, which allows some time to deal with anything that is urgent before the end of the day. If your email account allows it, have an auto responder email that tells senders that you review emails at specific times during the day. Suggest that if the matter is urgent and needs an immediate response to telephone you.

2. Consider implementing a time limit when responding and acknowledging emails when you do not have time to send an in-depth reply.

3. Include the original email in your reply by clicking "reply with history" as this will act as a reminder to the originator of the email.

4. When responding to an email, consider quoting from the original message by breaking it down into paragraphs and commenting on each point.

5. If forwarding the email to a third party to deal with, ensure that you inform the sender so that they know who will be responding to their email.

6. If someone has "blasted" you with an angry email, do not respond immediately. It will be tempting to respond by rebutting each point raised, instead consider a brief response.

7. Prioritise emails by looking at the subject line. So many emails that come into in boxes have been sent "blanket" to all staff but apply to only a few people. This is why it is important that when you send an email you have a meaningful subject line, because your recipient may be using a prioritisation system too.

8. Consider what action you will take upon receipt of an email; respond, retain, print off or delete. An approach to dealing

with paperwork can be easily transferred to dealing with emails. This is where, for any piece of paper you pick up, you will either action yourself, delegate, file or bin. When you first read the email decide whether it is urgent and important, and can only be dealt with by you. If it is important but not urgent, file it electronically. If it is less important can you delegate it? Finally, if it is neither important nor urgent then send it to the trash.

9. Think before you forward an email that has already been forwarded several times, especially where the original message is in the very first email. Consider copying and pasting the information into a new email. This also applies if there is an attachment. Take the time to save it and then attach it to a new email.

10. Where the email sender has sent email to several recipients, consider whether you need to use the "reply to all" button.

11. Consider using the junk mail facility. This is particularly useful when you are part of an email group and therefore end up receiving emails that have nothing to do with you.

12. Organise your emails by creating electronic folders for emails and word folders for attachments. You can set up

your emails to go directly into the specified folder; however, you need to be organised to check all the relevant folders.

13. Use colour coding to help you to distinguish between senders. This will help you quickly pick out the emails you want to deal with quickly.

14. Use the "out of office" feature when you know you will be away from the office. Tell people what you want them to do in your absence. If you are brave, leave a message stating that because of the large amount of emails you are likely to receive upon your return, you will delete all messages. Ask them to send the original message again after the date of your return.

12 Absolute Email Don'ts

1. Avoid using personal comments in official emails, especially when referring to clients.

2. When sharing an opinion or judgement, make sure it is relevant to the issue and not stated as fact.

3. Avoid writing in capitals as this is the equivalent of SHOUTING.

4. Do not send emails that are offensive or threatening in anyway.

5. Do not respond to an email if you are angry.

6. Do not send or forward chain letters.

7. Do not criticise people's grammar or spelling.

8. Do not send information by email which you know may be upsetting or unpleasant.

9. Be careful about making off hand or unguarded remarks.

10. Do not keep emails longer than you need.

11. Don't be tempted to check your emails every few minutes. Schedule times during the day when you will check emails in between other tasks.

12. Don't be afraid to give feedback. If you are receiving messages that you do not want, for example, jokes; respond politely asking that they stop.

5 Easy Steps To getting control of your inbox (Inbox Zero)

The purpose of inbox zero is for you to see the emails you have to take action on. I first learnt about inbox zero from David Allen, the author of *Getting Things Done – the art of stress-free productivity.*

0. Pre-step

Before we launch into the 5 step process, I want to show you how to reach inbox zero in just a few seconds, even if you have hundreds or thousands of emails in your inbox. If you have just returned from a period of leave or sickness, this is where you must start. You don't have to deal with the backlog whilst watching new emails land in your inbox.

Don't worry; we've not started step one 1 yet. This is a strategy that I adapted and works for me. I think it may work for you too. Create a folder and call it "backlog." You can call it what you like. Select all the emails in your inbox and move them into this new folder.

Now you have an empty inbox. Any emails that come in from this point you can implement the 5 steps below. You can go into your folder labelled "backlog" and use the 5 step process below to deal with them. You can do this all in one go or schedule time over the next few days to get through your backlog of emails.

1. Delete

This is something you must get into the habit of doing. For some reason it seems to be much easier to just leave emails festering in the inbox rather than deal with them. The emails in your inbox may not be taking up much physical space but each time you open your email to a full inbox it will feel as if they are occupying physical space in your brain.

If there is no action associated to the email and you don't need it for future reference, get rid of it. Take it out of your inbox. Delete is number one for a reason. This is your default position. Don't worry if you delete by accident. Just go over to the trash and retrieve it.

2. File

Up until today you have been using your inbox as your to-do list. That has to stop now. Now there will be some emails that you will want to keep for future reference. There are those that you won't be too sure about.

If you choose to keep either of these emails in your inbox you will soon lose track of them amongst the hundreds of other emails you've been keeping for a rainy day.

You just need to store them in a folder that is not your inbox. The simplest way to do this is to create a folder and name it "reference". In the future you should be able to find it by entering a keyword in the search box within your email. If you need a more sophisticated filing system you can create folders by topic, name of person, etc.

3. **Do under 2 minute tasks now**

   This is where you can operate the 2 minute rule. If the task is going to take you less than 2 minutes to complete, do it now. Just like a strategy used for dealing with post or a physical inbox; a piece of paper should be dealt with only once.

   You probably already scan/read emails and look at them again later to decide what to do with them. You may in fact read the same email several times before you actually action it. This is a waste of your time. It takes time to read an email and decide to do nothing with it. Those few seconds build up over time.

   Get into the habit of reading an email once. Assess whether or not you can deal with that email in less than 2 minutes. You'll find that often many will need only a 30 second response.

4. Action

If you've been systematic and followed the above 3 steps, you should be left with emails that require some type of action and will take more than 2 minutes. There are two categories here. For this step we focus on those emails that require you to take the next step.

Create a folder and name it "Action". This is where you put those emails that you are responsible for taking the next action step. If there is a time connected to the action you must record that in whatever calendar system you use.

5. Waiting for

This is the second category related to those emails that require an action that will take more than 2 minutes. Here you are waiting for someone else to complete an action before you take it forward. Again create a folder and name it "Waiting For".

Once you have notification that the action you are waiting for has been completed, you go through the process above. Can you delete it? Do you need to keep it for reference? Are you required to take some kind of action?

Conclusion

I hope this book has been useful. If there is only one thing that you have taken away from this book and implemented, I have done my job.

Having read the book, you will know this is not so much a book about record keeping but more about taking responsibility of what you have within your control. When you are totally overwhelmed with work it is very easy to feel that things are out of your control.

Record keeping just happens to be one of those tasks that gets marginalised when you have far too much work to do and not enough time to do it in. When things go wrong, record keeping is the first thing that is looked at and interrogated.

The main purpose of this book is to give you back the power. It is not about giving you the tools to squeeze even more work out of less and less time. It is about you working smarter, not harder. It is about you leaving work on time. It is about you getting to the end of your day and feeling that you have accomplished something. It is about you getting home and being fully present for your family. It is about you having a life and enjoying life, so that when you return to work the next day you are ready to give your all once again.

References

Allen, D (2001) Getting Things Done: How To Achieve Stress-Free Productivity. Piatkus

Goldsmith, L. (1999). Recording with Care. What People Say and What Needs to Be Done. [Online] Available from: http://webarchive.nationalarchives.gov.uk/+/www.dh.gov.uk/en/P ublicationsandstatistics/Publications/PublicationsPolicyAndGuid ance/DH_4010129. [Accessed: 23 April 2013)

Forster, M (2000). Get Everything Done And Still Have Time To Play. Hoddler & Stoughton

O'Rourke, L. (2010). Recording in Social Work: Not just an administrative task. The Policy Press.

Covey, S (2004). The 7 Habits Of Highly Effective People. Simon & Schuster Ltd

United Kingdom. Department for Children, Schools and Families and Communities and Local Government. (2008). Information Sharing: Pocket Guide. [Online] Available from:

https://www.education.gov.uk/publications/eOrderingDownload/ 00808-2008BKT-EN-March09.pdf. [Accessed: 23 April 2013]

United Kingdom. Social Work Inspectorate. (2010). Practice Guide: On The Record – Getting It Right: Effective Management of Social Work Recording. [Online]

Available from: http://www.gov.scot/Resource/Doc/299693/0093435.pdf . [Accessed: 31 August 2015]

Printed in Poland
by Amazon Fulfillment
Poland Sp. z o.o., Wrocław